**Working with
Behavioral Disorders**

Teaching Students with Behavioral Disorders:

Basic Questions and Answers

Timothy J. Lewis, Juane Heflin,
and Samuel A. DiGangi

A Product of the ERIC Clearinghouse on Handicapped and Gifted Children
Published by The Council for Exceptional Children

Library of Congress Cataloging-in-Publication Data

Lewis, Timothy, 1960-
   Teaching students with behavioral disorders : basic questions and
answers / Timothy Lewis, Juane Heflin, Samuel A. DiGangi.
       p.   cm. — (Working with behavioral disorders)
   "CEC mini-library."
   "A product of the ERIC Clearinghouse on Handicapped and Gifted
Children."
   Includes bibliographical references (p.).
   ISBN 0-86586-205-2
   1. Handicapped children—Education—United States. 2. Handicapped
children—Education—United States—Curricula. I. Heflin, Juane.
II. DiGangi, Samuel A. III. Council for Exceptional Children.
IV. ERIC Clearinghouse on Handicapped and Gifted Children.
V. Title. VI. Series.
LC4031.L48   1991
371.93—dc20   91-12022
                                                                     CIP

ISBN 0-86586-205-2

A product of the ERIC Clearinghouse on Handicapped and Gifted Children

Published in 1991 by The Council for Exceptional Children, 1920 Association
Drive, Reston, Virginia 22091-1589.
Stock No. P337

This publication was prepared with funding from the U.S. Department of
Education, Office of Educational Research and Improvement, contract no.
RI88062007. Contractors undertaking such projects under government sponsor-
ship are encouraged to express freely their judgment in professional and
technical matters. Prior to publication the manuscript was submitted for critical
review and determination of professional competence. This publication has met
such standards. Points of view, however, do not necessarily represent the
official view or opinions of either The Council for Exceptional Children or the
Department of Education.

Printed in the United States of America
10 9 8 7 6 5 4 3 2 1

Contents

Do curricular decisions change as the student enters adolescence?

When should instructional emphasis shift to focus on vocational skills?

Should teachers use different instructional strategies for withdrawn vs. aggressive students?

Which instructional techniques are most appropriate?

What criteria can be used to decide whether or not a particular curriculum is appropriate and how do I procure materials on a limited budget?

How are social skills best taught?

How can student's goals and objectives be best used in planning curricula? How much documentation is necessary in terms of student progress toward objectives?

What nonaversive strategies are most effective in changing behaviors?

Does medication help calm students?

How long does it take to tell whether or not a new strategy is working?

What are the danger signs of potentially explosive situations? What consequences are appropriate for aggressive behavior?

How should teachers prepare students for the mainstream?

How can teachers design instruction to promote a positive classroom environment?

How can teachers avoid stress and possible burnout?

Where can teachers find help in dealing with problems such as substance abuse, AIDS, or suspected child abuse?

Related Reading, 28

3. Collaboration for Success, 30

Collaborating with Other Teachers and Paraprofessionals
What are some effective strategies for developing good working relationships?

How can teachers of students with behavioral disorders increase regular staff understanding?

How can mainstreaming be achieved?

How can the teacher of students with behavioral disorders effectively assist the regular education teacher?

Collaborating with Administrators

What can be done to increase the awareness of administrators, legislators, and the community?

What skills do teachers need to deal effectively with administrative requests?

What can be done when the budget falls short?

Collaborating with the Community

How can a support network be established?

What happens when a student is arrested and incarcerated?

Collaborating with Parents

Where can teachers refer parents who seek help in working with their children?

What communication techniques facilitate good parent/teacher relationships?

How can teachers promote the generalization of positive change into the home environment?

How can the educational system meet the needs of students given the restraints of a difficult home life?

Related Reading, 37

Foreword

Working with Behavioral Disorders
CEC Mini-Library

One of the greatest underserved populations in the schools today is students who have severe emotional and behavioral problems. These students present classroom teachers and other school personnel with the challenges of involving them effectively in the learning process and facilitating their social and emotional development.

The editors have coordinated a series of publications that address a number of critical issues facing service providers in planning and implementing more appropriate programs for children and youth with severe emotional and behavioral problems. There are nine booklets in this Mini-Library series, each one designed for a specific purpose.

- *Teaching Students with Behavioral Disorders: Basic Questions and Answers* addresses questions that classroom teachers commonly ask about instructional issues, classroom management, teacher collaboration, and assessment and identification of students with emotional and behavioral disorders.

- *Conduct Disorders and Social Maladjustments: Policies, Politics, and Programming* examines the issues associated with providing services to students who exhibit externalizing or acting-out behaviors in the schools.

- *Behaviorally Disordered? Assessment for Identification and Instruction* discusses systematic screening procedures and the need for functional assessment procedures that will facilitate provision of services to students with emotional and behavioral disorders.

- *Preparing to Integrate Students with Behavioral Disorders* provides guidelines to assist in the integration of students into mainstream settings and the delivery of appropriate instructional services to these students.

- *Teaching Young Children with Behavioral Disorders* highlights the applications of Public Law 99–457 for young children with special needs and delineates a variety of interventions that focus on both young children and their families.

- *Reducing Undesirable Behaviors* provides procedures to reduce undesirable behavior in the schools and lists specific recommendations for using these procedures.

- *Social Skills for Students with Autism* presents information on using a variety of effective strategies for teaching social skills to children and youth with autism.

- *Special Education in Juvenile Corrections* highlights the fact that a large percentage of youth incarcerated in juvenile correctional facilities has special learning, social, and emotional needs. Numerous practical suggestions are delineated for providing meaningful special education services in these settings.

- *Moving On: Transitions for Youth with Behavioral Disorders* presents practical approaches to working with students in vocational settings and provides examples of successful programs and activities.

We believe that this Mini-Library series will be of great benefit to those endeavoring to develop new programs or enhance existing programs for students with emotional and behavioral disorders.

Lyndal M. Bullock
Robert B. Rutherford, Jr.

Introduction

The purpose of this book is to provide educators who work with students who display challenging behaviors with professionally sound information to improve their effectiveness. The format is a series of questions and answers generated by preservice and inservice teachers who plan to work or are currently working with students with behavioral disorders. The answers are based on research and applied literature representing current best practices and are designed to assist special and regular educators who have limited preparation or experience in working with students with behavioral problems. For the purpose of this book, the term *students with behavioral disorders (BD)* will be used to denote students who may be categorized as "seriously emotionally disturbed," "emotionally disordered," "behaviorally disabled," or having another, similar disability.

The list of over 100 questions, generated by both teachers and teachers in training, are grouped into three separate sections. "Effective Assessment and Evaluation Practices" focuses on questions and answers relating to the assessment of students who display behavior problems—for both the classification of such students and diagnostic information for the development of instructional interventions.

"Developing Curriculum and Instruction for Students with Behavioral Disorders" focuses on designing intervention strategies to change academic and social behaviors. The most effective tools available for practitioners are qualitative teaching strategies. Throughout this section, emphasis is placed on developing instructional strategies that focus on increasing positive behaviors, as opposed to exclusively focusing on reducing negative behaviors.

"Collaboration for Success" looks at issues surrounding the development of positive partnerships with other professionals and parents to better educate students with behavioral disorders. This section is divided into four areas addressing collaboration with (a) other teachers and paraprofessionals, (b) administrators, (c) community agencies outside the school setting, and (d) parents.

At the end of each section, a list of related references is provided for further information. Most of the references are directly concerned with the education of students with behavioral disorders. However, several of the citations focus on educational services for all students with disabilities, but they are equally appropriate in the provision of services for students with behavioral disorders.

1. Effective Assessment and Evaluation Practices

The purpose of assessment and evaluation is to determine the most effective instructional interventions for specific students. *Assessment* involves gathering information by means of conducting observations, administering tests, and recording interview responses. The questions addressed in this section promote a functional approach to assessment of student behavior.

Evaluation is the process of comparing the student's behavior to a standard and noting the discrepancy (Howell & Morehead, 1987). The standard serves as the desired behavior, representing what the evaluator feels the student "should be doing." The evaluator's standard is influenced by factors such as the behavior of other students, societal beliefs, classroom norms, and categorical definitions. For the purpose of comparison and evaluation, the standard should represent the level of functioning required for the student to be successful at specific tasks.

Two types of decisions can be made from assessment information: classification decisions and treatment decisions. *Classification decisions* include the assignment of categorical labels such as "behaviorally disordered," "mentally retarded," "learning disabled"; placement in special service programs, assignment to grade levels; and so forth. *Treatment decisions* include "what-to-teach" and "how-to-teach" decisions. The decisions addressed in this section focus primarily on assessment and evaluation for the purpose of making treatment decisions—the types of decisions made by teachers.

The procedures detailed here can be applied when evaluating academic as well as social-behavioral concerns. In essence, effective evaluation and remediation incorporate tenets of task-analysis, data-based decision making, curriculum-based assessment, and applied behavior analysis. The result is a series of approaches that can be employed in the classroom to address student learning and instruction effectively and efficiently.

The responses to each of the questions reflect the belief that all students can learn when provided with effective instruction.

What are appropriate techniques?

Student behavior can be evaluated with respect to various performance standards and through a variety of observation approaches. Ideally, a functional analysis of student behavior (detailed elsewhere in this document) via multimethod approaches to assessment should be adopted. This approach to evaluating student behavior may incorporate ratings and views of student behavior or academic performance from the perspectives of several people involved with the student: the student's teacher, other teachers in the school, the student's parents, peers, and the student himself or herself may serve as rater or evaluator of the target behavior.

A data-based approach should be employed when evaluating students with behavioral disorders. Direct observations and recordings of the students' ongoing performance will assist in making instructional decisions. The following points should be considered when devising an evaluation approach.

- There should be a clear purpose for testing.
- If items or questions are presented, each item should be keyed to an objective.
- Objectives should be defined operationally and should clearly state the four necessary components: learner, condition, behavior, and criteria.
- The measure should assess the strategies needed to perform the objective successfully.
- The measure should provide an adequate sample of student behavior.
- The measure should be presented in an appropriate format.
- The measure should be easy to use and interpret.

How should the teacher establish expectations?

Teacher expectations represent the goals for which a teacher holds the students accountable. These goals or expectations serve as a standard by which the teacher assesses the students' current performance or functioning. Teachers hold both academic and social behavioral expectations for their students. For students in regular classrooms, teacher expectations center on the behaviors necessary for successful participation in adult life. Expectations for students with behavioral disorders should ultimately be the same as those established for their nondisabled peers.

Special educators often focus on *individualization of instruction,* which refers to the efforts made to ensure that each student is receiving instruction that meets his or her needs. This does not mean that these students are held to a lesser expectation of performance. However, short-term expectations may have to be adjusted to account for the student's current level of performance and the path to the goal may have to be broken into more specific steps. The expected date of mastery or amount of time necessary to accomplish a given skill may require an increase for some students. The critical point is that the expectations or ultimate goals are not altered for students with behavioral problems. Evaluation of student progress, as well as evaluation of the effectiveness of interventions, centers on the student's making progress that will permit attainment of both short- and long-term goals.

Establishing ultimate expectations should be no more difficult for students in special education than for students in regular classrooms. Evaluations are, in essence comparing student behavior to the evaluator's expectation or standard. It may be best to view "expectations" as short-term goals and long-term goals. Long-term goals are the curriculum objectives that are in place for *all* students. The curriculm is not changed for students in special education. If it represents skills that the society, the community, the teachers, parents, and students hold as important, then *all* students should have the opportunity to move toward these objectives. However, the process by which they meet goals or expectations may vary among students. The following points are important to keep in mind when setting expectations for students with behavioral problems:

- Use data-based decision rules to guide instructional decisions.

- Do not change or lower curriculum expectations for students in special education. They also need the opportunity to receive instruction geared toward optimizing their progress toward those goals.

- Assess the student's competence at prerequisite subskills and strategies for combining those subskills to perform the task.

- Use continuous performance monitoring to assess the student's progress toward the goal.

- Adjust teaching accordingly when the student strays from the projected path toward the goal.

- Employ direct instruction of the necessary subskills and strategies.

- Realize that accuracy is only one way that a student may demonstrate proficiency at a task. Focus on teaching higher-level thinking skills (e.g., strategies for combining subskills to perform other tasks or strategies for recognizing environmental cues and monitoring the appropriateness of one's own prosocial behavior) to bring the student to mastery and automaticity levels.

Does the student's disorder cause the problem behavior?

Even though the source of a student's problem behavior may be related to the identified or underlying "disorder," attempts to validate this assumption may be of limited educational relevance. If rigorous assessment procedures resulted in the identification of a disorder that "explains" the student's behavior, the next step would be to remediate the behavior. Research has shown that the most effective way to remediate academic and prosocial deficits is through direct instruction of the target skill. The effective approach to remediation of behavioral problems is to pinpoint the area of concern, generate an operational definition, and conduct the evaluation procedures detailed here.

Students with behavioral disorders exhibit behavior that is different from that of our standard, or the curriculum. The behavior problem may or may not be caused by an internal deficit or disorder. Addressing and remediating the problem ultimately involves efforts to identify it, teach the necessary subskills or strategies, and measure student performance toward mastery of those skills and strategies.

How can behavioral rating scales be incorporated into the curriculum?

Behavioral rating scales can be used to assess and compare a student's behavior to a list of "ideal" behaviors. The student's mastery of these skills can also be compared to other students' mastery to assist in identifying common areas of deficit in prosocial skills performance in the classroom. In this way, rating scales can assist the teacher in selecting target skills for instructional intervention. Rating scales can also provide the teacher with a systematic approach for assessing changes in an individual student's behavior as a result of an intervention plan.

The use of multiple ratings of student behavior can ensure the social validity of the intervention as well as provide a means for assessing the generalization of learning to different areas. Rating scales completed by multiple observers cawn provide a means for assessing the social validity of an intervention—the appropriateness of the targeted behavior from the standpoint of others in the student's environment.

Following are three behavior rating scales that may be useful in assessing student behavior:

Behavior Dimension Rating Scale (BDRS)
L. M. Bullock and M. J. Wilson
DLM Teacher Resources
One DLM Park
Allen, TX 75002

Behavior Evaluation Scale (BES)
S. McCarney, J. Leigh, and J. Cornbleet
Associated Management Systems
P. O. Box 510
Vernon, AL 35592

Walker Problem Behavior Identification-Revised (WPBI-R)
H. M. Walker
Western Psychological Services
12031 Wilshire Boulevard
Los Angeles, CA 90025

What is the least restrictive environment for these students?

The least restrictive environment (LRE) is the setting that best meets the needs of the student. The term is often interpreted as a mandate that students with disabilities be mainstreamed in regular classrooms. For students with behavioral disorders, regular classroom placement is often the environment where the most learning can take place. For some students, however, resource room programs are determined to be the LRE, and for others, self-contained special education classrooms may be required. Determination of the LRE is a primary component of all placement decisions. The determination is not made by one individual and the decision is not based on any one specific criterion. A multidisciplinary team, often comprised of a special education teacher, the student's regular education teacher, school psychologist, parents, and other professionals associated with the student makes decisions regarding the program that will best meet an individual student's needs. In determining the LRE, the following points should be addressed:

- Which placement will result in the most growth for the student both academically and socially?
- Can the designated placement meet the student's needs?
- Does the placement provide interaction with nondisabled students while ensuring academic success?

Does the least restrictive environment produce positive effects?

By definition, the LRE is the placement in which the student most benefits from instruction. The requirement that a student with behavioral problems be placed in the least restrictive environment ensures that the students' needs are met in the best possible way. Often, the LRE for a student with behavioral problems is determined to be a regular classroom setting, perhaps with resource room support. The rationale behind this decision is based on research demonstrating that the most effective way to teach students behaviors that they are lacking is to expose them to others who demonstrate the behaviors. In the case of prosocial skills, it seems to follow that a student lacking age-appropriate interpersonal skills is more likely to benefit from exposure to students who demonstrate these skills than from exposure to students who lack the appropriate skills. This seemingly logical approach does not, however, ensure that the student will learn the appropriate skills merely by being exposed to them. Direct instruction on target skills is often required to ensure that students master them. Instruction on specific skills is often provided via resource room pullout programs, and at times through consultation between the regular classroom teacher and the special education teacher, the school psychologist, or other behavioral or instructional experts. To most effectively address the student's needs in the regular classroom, as well as ensure that the other students in the classroom benefit from instruction, the teacher should

- Keep an organized classroom learning environment.
- Provide an abundance of success for all of the students.
- Hold high expectations.
- Devise a structured behavior management program.
- Maintain close working relationships with the special education teacher and other staff members.
- Collect data so that the effects of instruction-based decisions can be evaluated and modified.

- Focus on teaching self-management and self-monitoring skills so that the student eventually becomes adept at monitoring natural cues and adjusts his or her own behavior.

Does the IEP help the teacher work with the student?

The answer to this question certainly depends upon the quality of the individualized education program (IEP). The IEP should provide specific instructional objectives for the student. These objectives should be operationally defined and directly observable. The criteria for acceptable performance should be stated in a measurable, countable form. The method of measuring the student's progress toward this goal should be clearly stated. In essence, the IEP provides a plan for both remediating and evaluating the effects of the intervention on student performance. It guides a teach-test-teach approach to intervention. Formulation of instructional decisions is based on a continuous monitoring of the student's progress toward the goals stated in the IEP.

The IEP also serves as a means of communicating the goals to the student's parents and teachers, the school psychologist, and others. In and of itself, the IEP does not ensure successful application of a special education program, but it does provide a means of communicating objectives and specifying intervention and evaluation procedures regarding the student. Each of these pieces of information provides important information about the student.

Information about a student's previous performance should not limit expectations for the student in the new placement setting. The amount of energy required to obtain the information should be proportional to its value in making instructional decisions. Talking to past teachers, parents, and school psychologists can provide valuable information. However, these sources might also provide a distorted picture of what is actually taking place. Therefore, it is important to take into consideration interventions that have been tried in the past, as well as situations in which the student performed successfully or demonstrated appropriate behavior.

Is a student with a conduct disorder different from one with a behavioral disorder?

The debate over provision of services continues among administrators, special interest groups, parents, and others concerned with the education of students with behavioral problems. At present, differences in semantics and interpretations of definitions may result in differences in categorical labels. Given two students who demonstrate unacceptable behavior, one may qualify for special education services, while the other is to receive services from the regular classroom teacher. The decision as to whether or not to exclude a student from special education services may not be the immediate concern of the regular classroom teacher or special educator. Students who are referred to as "conduct disordered" and students who are referred to as "emotionally disabled," "behaviorally disordered," "seriously emotionally disturbed," or "emotionally and behaviorally disordered" have two common elements that are instructionally relevant: (1) they demonstrate behavior that is noticeably different from that expected in school or the community and (2) they are in need of remediation.

In each instance, the student is exhibiting some form of behavior that is judged to be different from that which is expected in the classroom. The best way to approach a student with a "conduct disorder" and a student with a "behavioral disorder" is to operationally define exactly what it is that each student does that is discrepant with the expected standard. Once it has been expressed in terms of behaviors that can be directly observed, the task of remediation becomes clearer. A student's verbally abusive behavior can be addressed, whereas it is difficult to directly identify or remediate a student's "conduct disorder," since that term may refer to a variety of behaviors of widely different magnitudes. The most effective and efficient approach is to pinpoint the specific behavioral problem and apply data-based instruction to remediate it.

Related Reading

Goldstein, A. P., Sprafkin, R. P., Gershaw, N. J., & Klein, P. (1980). *Skillstreaming the adolescent.* Champaign, IL: Research Press.

Howell, K. W., & Kaplan, J. S. (1980). *Diagnosing basic skills: A handbook for deciding what to teach.* Columbus, OH: Merrill.

Howell, K. W., & Morehead, M. K. (1987). *Curriculum-based evaluation for special and remedial education.* Columbus, OH: Merrill.

Kaplan, J. S. (1991). *Beyond behavior modification: A cognitive-behavioral approach to behavior management in the school.* Austin, TX: Pro-Ed.

Kerr, M. M., & Nelson, C. M. (1983). *Strategies for managing behavior problems in the classroom.* Columbus, OH: Merrill.

McGinnis, F., & Goldstein, A. P. (1984). *Skillstreaming the elementary school child.* Champaign, IL: Research Press.

Rutherford, R. B., Jr., & Nelson, C. M. (1988). Applied behavior analysis in education: Generalization and maintenance. In J. C. Witt, S. N. Eliott, & F. M. Gresham (Eds.), *Handbook of behavior therapy in education* (pp. 125–153). New York: Plenum.

Strickland, B. B., & Turnbull, A. P. (1990). *Developing and implementing individualized education programs* (3rd ed.). Columbus, OH: Merrill.

2. Developing Curriculum and Instruction for Students with Behavioral Disorders

This section discusses issues related to developing and implementing curriculum and instruction in classrooms serving students with behavioral problems. Throughout the section, a teaching approach is advocated to change both academic and social behaviors (Wolery, Bailey, & Sugai, 1988). Several common themes should be kept in mind. First, all instructional decisions, for both academic and social behavior, should be based on each student's individual needs. Second, all instructional decisions should be data-based to ensure efficient and effective instruction. Finally, for children who display either externalizing or internalizing behavior problems, it is important to focus on the positive alternatives to the problem behavior when developing curriculum and behavioral interventions. In other words, when writing objectives and developing interventions, the key question to bear in mind is "What do I want the student to do in place of the problem behavior?"

What is the optimal teacher-to-student ratio for effective instruction? Should self-contained classes include a wide range of ages and skill levels?

There is no optimal teacher-to-student ratio that can be applied to all classrooms. The optimal number will vary according to such factors as the severity of the disabling conditions of the students, the type of classroom in which students receive instruction (self-contained vs. resource), and whether or not qualified teaching assistants are available. In order to determine the most effective ratio, the critical question teachers must ask themselves is "Can I meet the academic and behavioral needs of all of my students?" Ideally, the teacher will have either a homogeneous group of students—one in which all students are close in age and academic ability—or qualified assistants who will enable the teacher to divide a heterogeneous classroom into small groups of students with similar academic and behavioral needs.

In reality, this ideal classroom is not often the case. Teachers are faced with caseloads of students who vary in age, academic ability, and severity of disabling condition, with little or no assistance. If this is the case, the following recommendations will assist the teacher in meeting the needs of all of his or her students:

- Teach students in small groups according to their present academic level of performance.

- If teaching assistants are not available to concurrently conduct small academic groups, provide remaining students with independent activities through learning centers.

- If the class contains students with a wide range of ages, schedule mainstream classes and activities such as lunch and recess with similar-aged peers to provide an opportunity for students with behavioral disorders to interact with those peers.

- Solicit the help of volunteers to supervise small groups or provide one-to-one instruction.

Which curriculum should be stressed, academics or social behavior?

As with all curriculum decisions, the teacher should design instruction to meet the individual needs of the students. For most students with behavior problems, both academic and social behavior changes will be needed. Two important components of any program that will effectively address both academic and social behavioral concerns are effective teaching strategies and an effective behavior management system.

Effective teaching strategies have proved to optimize the academic performance of students with disabilities. Enabling a student to be academically successful often leads to fewer behavioral problems in the classroom. Likewise, an effective behavior management system will lead to fewer behavior problems, thereby enabling the student to perform better academically. In other words, curricular choices should be made based on the student's needs, and they will be most beneficial and motivational if used in conjunction with effective teaching strategies and effective behavior management systems.

Do curricular decisions change as the student enters adolescence?

The instructional objectives to be addressed are related to both the curriculum objectives and the individual student's current placement in the curriculum. The curriculum in this sense serves as a series of skills. It is not changed for students with behavioral problems. The areas of focus and the sophistication of focus on specific prosocial skills and strategies may be adapted to best meet the needs of adolescents with behavioral problems. Generally, instruction at the secondary school level should address four areas: academics, social behaviors, vocational skills, and postschool transition. In most cases, problem behavior has interfered with the student's opportunity to learn. Therefore, academic instruction is likely to be necessary in order to bring the student to mastery of essential skills. A curriculum-based program should be implemented, employing continuous monitoring of student progress to guide instructional decisions. Frequent measures of the skills being taught will provide the teacher with the necessary information for making data-based instructional decisions.

Another area of concern is prosocial skills. Teaching social skills to students with behavioral disorders is of the utmost concern since the very fact that these students have been labeled "behaviorally disordered" is likely an indicator that they do not exhibit appropriate prosocial behavior. In addition to applying the procedures for determining what to teach and how to measure mastery of targeted skills, instruction focusing on self-management is particularly relevant with adolescents who demonstrate behavioral problems. As students prepare to leave the structured environment of the school, it is critical that their behavior be under the control of naturally occurring environmental cues. They should be provided instruction addressing self-management of behavior, including self-monitoring, assessing environmental cues, making decisions regarding appropriate context for behavior, and so forth. The emphasis of the instructional program should not focus solely on social skills, but on the decision to apply and demonstrate those skills across settings.

Appropriate social behavior will impact the third and fourth areas of concern, vocational skills and postschool transitions. Secondary special education programs must also address the needs of students as they prepare to graduate or move into alternative programs. Academic and prosocial skills necessary for successful performance in the area in which the student may seek employment following high school should be addressed directly.

When making decisions regarding skills to be addressed at the secondary level, the following points should be considered:

- Treat each student individually, but compare performance to a criterion.
- Provide instruction in academic areas that are not at grade level.
- Provide instruction in social skills to enhance the opportunity for successful social interactions with others.
- Provide instruction in vocational skills to provide a successful future career.
- Provide basic survival skills to ensure a smooth transition into postschool life.

When should instructional emphasis shift to focus on vocational skills?

Although research has not indicated a specific appropriate grade level at which to include vocational concerns in a student's instructional program, the emphasis usually shifts earlier in the school careers of students with special needs. In regular education, entry into high school is accompanied by decisions regarding career directions. Students decide whether to take college preparatory courses, general education classes, specialized vocational/trade programs, or community-based alternative programs. The decision to divert attention from the traditional academic curriculum and focus on vocational training takes place at different points within special education programs. The most notable difference between the special and regular education focus on vocational concerns occurs with instruction provided to students who have mental retardation. For these students, a vocational or community-based approach to education may supplant a traditional academic emphasis much earlier than in regular education so that they will be adequately prepared for a vocation at graduation.

The level at which to make the decision to address vocational skills in programs for students with behavioral disorders is not as clear. In determining the focus of a student's instructional program, it is necessary to keep in mind that the student must be provided with instruction relevant to the curriculum objectives that ensure success in society. The objectives that are covered in elementary-school-level curricula contribute to later vocational adjustment. Mastery of concepts such as money, vocabulary, time, and measurement relationships is essential for vocational success. The stronger the academic base, the more opportunities the student will have with regard to future career choices. From an academic perspective, basic subskills and strategies necessary for mastery of higher-level skills should be addressed. A vocational or community-based approach to education enables the student to be adequately prepared for a vocation at graduation.

To ensure vocational success for students with behavioral problems, vocational instruction should address (a) career choices, (b) basic competencies required in the work environment, (c) safety procedures, and (d) familiarity with community assistance organizations, or where to go for help outside of the school setting. The focus for vocational skill instruction should include the following:

- Development of positive work habits and values.
- Social skill development.
- Career awareness.
- Job skills.
- Daily living skills.
- The overall concept of work, both as consumer and producer.

Should teachers use different instructional strategies for withdrawn vs. aggressive students?

Two questions need to be addressed in developing any behavior change procedure regardless of the student's current behavioral difficulty: What do I want the student to do instead?" and "What is the most effective and efficient means to help the student reach his or her goals?" Regardless of whether the student is withdrawn or aggressive, the objective is to exhibit a prosocial response instead of the current behavior. We may want the internalizing student to play with peers on the playground instead of playing alone. We may want the externalizing student to play appropriately with peers on the playground instead of hitting peers during games. For both behavior patterns, we have identified what we want them to do instead of the current problem behavior.

The next step is to develop interventions to help the students change their behavior. For students with either externalizing or internalizing behaviors, a direct teaching approach is advocated. This approach involves the four broad steps outlined below. Throughout the intervention, it is important to focus on the positive by emphasizing the prosocial replacement response rather than the original problem behavior.

- *Conduct the assessment.* This first step includes both a functional analysis and collection of baseline data on the student's prosocial replacement behavior (not the target problem behavior). A functional analysis involves recording all events and actions prior to and immediately following the students' behavior as they occur during specific time periods. (Most behavior management text books can provide examples and further instruction on conducting functional analyses.) Baseline data are objective observations of the student's present level of behavioral performance prior to intervening.

- *Develop objectives.* Once assessment is complete, the teacher will have data from which to develop a behavioral objective. The behavior specified in the objective should be the prosocial replacement behavior.

- *Develop and implement an intervention.* The intervention should be developed to teach the student a prosocial response in place of current behavior. Results of the functional analysis will lend insight into developing an appropriate intervention. For example, the externalizing student hits peers during games when he or she loses a turn or a peer laughs at a mistake. An appropriate intervention to address this problem might include teaching the student an alternate response and reward the student when the new response is used.

- *Evaluate the intervention.* By continuously collecting data throughout the intervention, the teacher can make sound decisions regarding the effectiveness of the intervention. The goal is to ensure that the student is making progress to meet his or her objectives.

Which instructional techniques are most appropriate?

Effective teaching practices will maximize the likelihood of student success. Effective teaching strategies are techniques that have been found to significantly increase student learning and decrease related behavioral problems. Following is a summary of key characteristics of effective classrooms broken into two groups, strategies for individual lessons and strategies to use throughout the school day:

INDIVIDUAL LESSON

- Clearly communicate to students the goal/purpose of the lesson.

- Present a well-organized, sequenced lesson.

- Use a "lead-model-test" strategy when presenting new material. First explain key concepts of the lesson (lead), demonstrate how to perform the skill of the lesson (model) through examples and nonexamples of the skill, and finally require the student to independently perform the skill (test).

- Give clear instructional feedback (explain why an answer/response is correct or incorrect).

- Begin each lesson with the expectation that the students can and will learn the new skill.

- Ensure student success in each lesson by programming to promote high rates of student accuracy.

- Use quick pacing during instruction.

THROUGHOUT THE SCHOOL DAY

- Prompt and provide smooth transitions between lessons and activities.

- Distribute opportunities to practice new skills.

- Use natural contingencies for student success (e.g., grades, verbal praise, privileges).

- Provide and focus on positive interactions with students.

What criteria can be used to decide whether or not a particular curriculum is appropriate and how do I procure materials on a limited budget?

When reviewing and or developing materials for use with students with behavior problems, several points should be considered. Are the materials age appropriate? Avoid using matterials designed for younger-aged students even though they may meet the academic level of the student. Do the materials simultaneously meet the skill level and interest of the student? Does the material complement other materials and/or learning activities? Is the material easy to implement? Materials that are difficult or time consuming to implement often disrupt the flow of the lesson and distract from its critical essence.

Obtaining teaching materials on a limited budget often requires additional work and imagination on the part of the teacher, but it can often lead to creative and meaningful lessons. The following is a list of suggestions for finding free or inexpensive teaching materials:

- Adapt regular education materials.
- Ask your district special education coordinator and other resource personnel.
- Exchange materials with other special educators.
- Check with local colleges or universities for special education material libraries.
- Look for samples or special offers at educational conferences.
- Check your local library for catalogs and the *Guide to Free and Inexpensive Materials,* which are readily available.
- Write to government offices for pamphlets or other free literature, posters, and materials.
- Consult your Chamber of Commerce for free literature or maps.
- Consult your local newspaper concerning educational programs its staff may have developed for use with the newspaper.
- Take advantage of the regional resource centers established by state education agencies.

How are social skills best taught?

Social skills deficits or problems can be viewed as errors in learning; therefore, the appropriate skills need to be taught directly and actively. It is important to base all social skill instructional decisions on individual student needs. In developing a social skill curriculum it is important to follow a systematic behavior change plan.

During assessment of a student's present level of functioning, two factors should be addressed. First, the teacher must determine whether the social skill problem is due to a *skill deficit* or a *performance deficit.* The teacher can test the student by directly asking what he or she would do or can have the student role play responses in several social situations (e.g., "A peer on the bus calls you a name. What should you do?"). If the student can give the correct response but does not display the behavior outside the testing situation, the social skill problem is probably due to a performance deficit. If the student cannot produce the socially correct response, the social skill problem may be due to a skill deficit. More direct instruction may be required to overcome the skill deficits, while a performance deficit may simply require increasing positive contingencies to increase the rate of displaying the appropriate social response. In addition, during assessment, it is important to identify critical skill areas in which the student is having problems.

Once assessment is complete, the student should be provided with direct social skill instruction. At this point, the teacher has the option of using a prepared social skill curriculum or developing one independently. (See "Related Reading" for examples of published social skill curricula.) It is important to remember that since no published curriculum will meet the needs of all students, it should be supplemented with teacher-developed or -modified lessons.

Social skill lessons are best implemented in groups of 3 to 5 students and optimally should include socially competent peers to serve as models. The first social skill group lesson should focus on three things: an explanation of why the group is meeting, a definition of what social skills are, and an explanation of what is expected of each student during the group. It may also be helpful to implement behavior management procedures for the group (i.e., contingencies for compliance and noncompliance).

For each social skill lesson, the "lead-model-test" approach is recommended. The following sample lesson outlines this format. The sample lesson is the first of four in teaching students to manage anger (Stop, Pick an Action, Go with Action, and Check).

LEAD

- Identify the skill for the lesson "What to do when you're angry."
- Define the skill "When I get angry my heart pounds."
  - Ask each student to state what happens when he or she gets angry.
- Define the prosocial response "When we feel angry the first thing we should do is *stop* what we are doing."
  - Ask each student what is the first thing to do when he or she is angry.
- Define possible ways of *stopping* (e.g., count to 10).
  - Ask students for possible ways to *stop*.

MODEL

- Demonstrate ways of stopping by setting up role plays in which you are the one who becomes angry. Prompt students to observe, and, following the role play, ask students whether or not you became angry and whether or not you *stopped*. Give several appropriate and inappropriate examples (e.g., yelling instead of *stopping*).

- – Be sure to include all students by asking them whether or not they observed you *stopping*.
- Have the students practice role play examples.
  - – Be sure to include all students by asking them whether or not they observed the students *stopping*.

TEST

- Set up new examples for each student to role play.
- Ask the students to state the skill learned (e.g., "What do you do when you get angry?").

It is important to prompt the students to use newly learned skills throughout the day and across settings to promote maintenance and generalization. It is also important to reinforce the students when they use new skills.

How can students' goals and objectives be best used in planning curricula? How much documentation is necessary in terms of student progress toward objectives?

Goals and objectives should focus on increasing or improving the student's present level of functioning and long-range planning (e.g., returning to mainstream, acceptance in vocational program, graduation). It is essential that the teacher write high-quality objectives.

Each objective written, academic or social, should contain the following four components:

1. *A learner*—Who.
2. *A condition*—Where or when.
3. *A behavior*—What.
4. *Criteria*—How much and for how long.

The following standard format includes all four components without undue wording:

(CONDITION)   (LEARNER)   (BEHAVIOR)
"When angry with a peer, Martin will use acceptable language to relate
(CRITERIA)
why he is angry 80% of the time for 5 consecutive days."

The following points should also be considered in developing objectives:

- The behavior specified in the objective is functional across settings.
- The criteria are realistic and achievable and will help the student progress.
- The behavior specified in the objective will benefit the student (i.e., it is socially valid to change the student's behavior).
- Maintenance and generalization objectives are included for each skill specified.
- Student and parent input is included.
- The objective is age appropriate.
- The objective is written positively (i.e., the behavior is what you want the student to do, not what the student should *not* do).

Ideally, the teacher will collect data daily on each student's progress toward meeting his or her objectives. This will ensure that the intervention developed to change the targeted behavior is not withdrawn too soon or implemented longer than necessary. At minimum, the teacher should take frequent probes of student progress. Once the objective has been met, it is still helpful to collect periodic data to ensure that the new behavior is being maintained and generalized.

What nonaversive strategies are most effective in changing behaviors?

While the debate continues as to which interventions using aversive strategies are appropriate or inappropriate for use with students who have disabilities, most professionals agree that positive interventions should always be tried first. With any positive intervention, the emphasis is on increasing prosocial behavior. Therefore, when the goal is to reduce an inappropriate behavior, it is critical to focus on what the student should do in place of the inappropriate behavior. The following are a few of the more common intervention procedures that do not involve using an aversive strategy.

- *Positive reinforcement.* This includes any object (e.g., stickers, coupons) or event (e.g., verbal praise, computer time) given contingently upon the student's displaying the desired prosocial behavior.

- *Differential reinforcement.* This technique combines positive reinforcement and extinction. The teacher can choose to positively reinforce the student when the student displays any appropriate behavior or specific behaviors. Extinction is the withholding of positive reinforcement while the student displays inappropriate behavior. It is important to remember that extinction does not mean simple ignoring by the teacher unless the teacher's attention is reinforcing to the student. The teacher may need to encourage peers to ignore inappropriate student behavior also.

- *Use of prompts.* In an effort to signal or remind the student what is expected, prompts are often helpful. Prompts can be verbal (reminders of goals or what is expected) or visual (posted rules). It is important to fade the use of prompts from the curriculum as soon as possible.

Does medication help calm students?

The treatment of behavioral problems with medication remains a controversial issue. Ultimately, it is important to realize that medication that may have a positive effect on student behavior does not teach the student new or appropriate prosocial skills. Regardless of whether the student is receiving medication, he or she will likely require direct instruction of the skill. Stimulant medications have been researched the most with children with behavioral disorders. These drugs (e.g., ritalin, cylert, dexedrine) do not stimulate some children, but have the opposite effect. Effects of stimulants appear as little as 1 hour after ingestion.

Research has shown that in some cases, medication in the appropriate dosage can produce positive effects on a student's attention and impulsivity. However, opponents raise questions regarding undesirable effects the medication can have on the student's perception of control. The student may attribute more power to the medication than to his or her own ability to control or monitor personal behavior. The development of self-management or self-monitoring skills may be hampered by the student's belief that he or she is not able to control personal behavior.

Others have raised concern over the ways in which the need for medication is determined. Instances in which teachers have recommended that parents seek medication for their children are not uncommon. This sort of recommendation is clearly outside of the role of the classroom teacher. From a teaching perspective, the best approach is to be aware of which students are receiving medication. Administration times, dosage problems, and inconsistencies in administration can have dramatic effects on student behavior. Observations such as these should be reported to the parents and the school medical staff immediately. Teachers should also document and report behaviors that may be side-effects of medication (e.g., falling asleep, becoming excessively thirsty or hungry, demonstrating tremors, or developing blank stares). From an instructional perspective, students with behavioral problems who receive medication should be evaluated and assessed using the approaches detailed in this book. A focus on identifying specific skills, evaluating performance, and directly addressing skill deficits will ensure that these students benefit from instruction.

How long does it take to tell whether or not a new strategy is working?

To ensure optimal effectiveness, it is important to base all instructional decisions on student data. By failing to make data-based decisions, the teacher risks withdrawing an effective intervention prematurely or extending an intervention too long. To assist in making data-based decisions, the teacher should collect data prior to and throughout the intervention and plot the data on a graph. A sample plan might be as follows.

Prior to intervening, the teacher should collect baseline data representing the student's current level of functioning. Based on where the student is presently performing, the next step is to develop an objective. Make certain the criteria in the objective are similar to the type of data collected (e.g., percentage correct, time on task). Based on baseline data and the objective criteria, the next step is to draw an "aim line" on the student's graph. This represents the desired rate of progress the student should make in order to meet the objective. Aim lines are drawn as follows:

1. Determine the aim date and aim rate based on the criteria expressed in the student's long-term objective. Draw an aim star (an A rightside up for an accelerating target, an A upside down for a decelerating target) at the desired rate and date intersection.

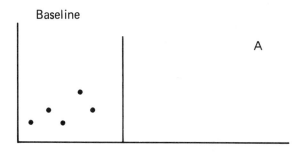

2. Determine the mid-date and mid-rate of the last 3 days of baseline data points. Mid-date and mid-rate are the median or middle-most points. For the mid-date, count left to right. For the mid-rate, count bottom to top.

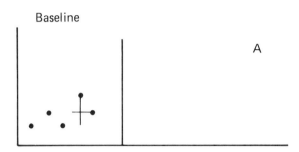

Baseline

A

3. Draw an aim line through the mid-date/mid-rate intersection to the aim star.

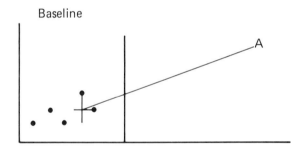

Baseline

A

4. Formulate "data decision rules." These rules indicate when the teacher should try an alternative intervention based on the student's graphed data pattern. A basic data decision rule for an objective that requires the student to increase a behavior might be stated as, "If the data fall below the aim line for 3 consecutive days, alter the current intervention."

What are the danger signs of potentially explosive situations? What consequences are appropriate for aggressive behavior?

Often, escalating, aggressive, or explosive behaviors occur in a predictable pattern or chain. Certain events or activities often precede the behavior outburst. It is therefore important for the teacher to identify potential "trouble spots" through direct observation. Common trouble spots for students with behavior problems include the following:

- Start-ups in lessons or activities.
- Transition times.
- Free or independent work times.
- Schedule disruptions.

When observing, the teacher should try to identify events that occur early in the sequence or chain; for example, noting what occurred just prior to the student's first displaying signs that his or her behavior might escalate to an outburst. Common behaviors that often occur early in the chain include the following:

- The student becomes unfocused from the task at hand.
- The student physically withdraws.
- The student takes a verbally or physically threatening posture.

The first step, then, should be one of prevention. The teacher can either rearrange the environment to avoid the trouble spots or provide the student with a prompt or verbal reminder of what behavior is expected during that time. Through social skill instruction, the teacher should also provide an appropriate alternative behavior for the student to engage in when confronted with trouble spots.

Once the student becomes upset and is displaying a behavior that could escalate, it is important for the teacher to intervene immediately to break the chain. The teacher should model appropriate anger control and avoid aggressive confrontations with the student. Ways to intervene include the following:

- Provide verbal prompts of expected behavior or reminders of the student's goals.
- Engage the student in problem-solving activities (previously taught to all students).
- Provide options for the student to avoid a negative situation (e.g., go to a quiet area, get a drink) and give the student a choice in selecting an option.

If the student's behavior continues to escalate and becomes aggressive or out of control, it is important to protect all students in the classroom. Try to avoid physical confrontations with the student when possible. An alternative to confronting the student in an attempt to remove him or her from the room is to remove the other students. This, of course, requires at least two adults, one to supervise the students who leave and the other to deal with the target student.

A set of consequences for behavior outbursts or aggressive behavior should be determined and in place before any instances actually occur. The procedures for handling out-of-control students and consequences should be put in writing and disseminated to all school personnel and parents.

How should teachers prepare students for the mainsteam?

If mainstreaming is a goal for a student with behavioral problems, it is important to plan for it. The process of preparing the student to be successful in the mainstream should begin when the student first receives special education services and continue after the student has been placed in the mainstream. Following are four broad phases that focus on promoting successful mainstreaming:

1. *Long-range planning*—While the student is receiving special education services.

    - At the initial and all subsequent IEP meetings, include maintenance and generalization objectives.

    - Use curriculum or instructional styles similar to those that are commonly found in the mainstream.

2. *Pre-Exit*—Prior to mainstreaming the student.

    - Assess the mainstream setting, through direct observation, for academic and behavioral demands.

    - Model special education instruction to match mainstream demands and teach key behaviors that will ensure success.

3. *Transition*—Integrating the student into the mainsteam.

    - Use a multidisciplinary team to make mainstream decisions in the same way as the team was used to place the student in special education (i.e., assess student's readiness, determine any needed resources).

    - Create timelines for transition. A gradual integration may be more beneficial to the student than an all-or-nothing approach.

4. *Follow-Up*—after the student is reintegrated into the mainsteam.

- Continue to collect data on the student's academic and behavioral progress to ensure that the student is maintaining progress and generalizing skills learned in the special education setting.
- Establish a mechanism for consultation with the regular educator.

How can teachers design instruction to promote a positive classroom environment?

Using effective teaching strategies will promote student academic and social behavioral success. Teachers should avoid focusing on students' inappropriate behavior and, instead, focus on desirable replacement behaviors. Focusing behavior management systems on positive, prosocial replacement responses will provide students with the opportunity to practice and be reinforced for appropriate behaviors. Above all else, have fun with students! Humor in the classroom lets students view school and learning as fun. Humor can also be used to avoid escalating behaviors by removing the negative focus from the problem.

How can teachers avoid stress and possible burnout?

The research on teacher burnout or attrition often points to two reasons given by teachers as to why they leave the field of behavioral disorders: (1) the amount of paperwork and administrative duties required outside the teaching day, and (2) the feeling of professional isolation.

Most paperwork, meetings, and conferences are either mandated by law or necessary to provide the best educational service to the population of students with BD. The more severe the disabling condition of a student the more personnel and agencies are involved in treatment delivery, placing additional administrative burdens on the teacher. The solution is to be aware of the administrative duties, seek support, and manage time effectively. To manage time effectively, the teacher should be willing to delegate certain duties to support personnel, for example, by relying on the teaching assistant to develop and implement lessons during the teacher's attendance at meetings. This requires planning. The teacher must make sure that the teaching assistant is aware of and able to implement the curriculum effectively. The supervisor or building administrator should grant monthly release time for teachers to complete paperwork, make site visits, or hold meetings.

More than other teachers of students with disabilities, teachers who work with students with behavioral disorders are often perceived as being distinctly associated with their students. Other teachers often are quick to point out misbehavior of "your" students to teachers in the BD field. By definition, students with severe emotional disabilities and/or behavioral disorders present daily emotional challenges to the classroom teacher. The association of student behavior with the teacher's instruction and the resulting daily stress often lead to a feeling of isolation from other teaching professionals. The answer is to seek support from among the following sources:

- Administrators.
- District consultants.
- School psychologists or counselors.
- Other special educators.
- Professional organizations such as The Council for Exceptional Children (CEC) and The Council for Children with Behavioral Disorders (CCBD).
- University practicum students.

While these resources directly address the most common reasons for burnout, teachers are also advised to take the following steps:

- Attend professional conferences and inservice training sessions.
- Separate personal from professional life.
- Set realistic goals for students and self.
- Participate in noneducational activities.
- Rotate class assignments with other special education teachers.
- Exercise.

Where can teachers find help in dealing with problems such as substance abuse, AIDS, or suspected child abuse?

In today's changing society, it is inevitable that teachers will encounter problems to which there are no standard answers. The best course of action is to ask for help from someone with expertise in the problem area. Possible sources include school administrators, school counselors, professional organizations that focus on the suspected problem area (check the telephone book for local chapters), and information clearing-houses such as the following:

The Council for Exceptional Children
1920 Association Drive
Reston, VA 22091
703-620-3660

Council of Chief State School Officers
HIV/AIDS Prevention Education Project
379 Hall of States
400 North Capital Street, NW
Washington, DC 20001
202-393-8159

National Information Center for Handicapped Children and Youth
    (NICHCY)
P.O. Box 1492
Washington, DC 20013
1-800-999-5599
(NICHCY will also provide a listing of other clearinghouses and organizations).

Related Reading

Carter, J., & Sugai, G. (1988). Teaching social skills. *TEACHING Exceptional Children, 20*(1), 68–71.

Colvin, G., & Sugai, C. (1989). *Managing escalating behavior.* Eugene, OR: Behavior Associates.

Donnellan, A. M., LaVigna, G. W., Negri-Shoultz, N., & Fassbender, L. L. (1988). *Progress without punishment: Effective approaches for learners with behavior problems.* New York: Teachers College Press.

Erickson, M. T. (1987). *Behavior disorders of children and adolescents.* Englewood Cliffs, NJ: Prentice-Hall.

Evens, W. H., Evans, S. S., & Shmid, R. E. (1989). *Behavior and instructional management: An ecological approach.* Boston: Allyn and Bacon.

Gallagher, P. A. (1979). *Teaching students with behavior disorders: Techniques for classroom instruction.* Denver: Love.

George, N., & Lewis, T. (1990). Exit assistance for special educators. *TEACHING Exceptional Children, 23*(2), 34–39.

Goldstein, A. P., Sprafkin, R. P., Gershaw, M. J., & Klein, P. (1980). *Skillstreaming the adolescent: A structured learning approach to teaching prosocial skills.* Champaign, IL: Research Press.

Grossman, H. (1990). *Trouble-free teaching: Solutions to behavior problems in the classroom.* Mountain View, CA: Mayfield.

Jackson, J. F., Jackson, D. A., & Monroe, C. (1983). *Getting along with others: Teaching social effectiveness to children.* Champaign, IL: Research Press.

Kauffman, J. M. (1989). *Characteristics of behavior disorders of children and youth* (4th ed.). Columbus, OH: Merrill.

Kerr, M. M., & Nelson, C. M. (1989). *Strategies for managing behavior problems in the classroom.* Columbus, OH: Merrill.

Lewis, T., DiGangi, S., & Sugai, G. (1990). Techniques to facilitate behavioral programming decisions. In *The Oregon Conference Monograph* (pp. 103–109). University of Oregon, Eugene: College of Education.

McGinnis, E., & Goldstein, A. P. (1984). *Skillstreaming the elementary school child: A guide for teaching prosocial skills.* Champaign, IL: Research Press.

McIntyre, T. (1989). *The behavior management handbook: Setting up effective behavior management systems.* Boston: Allyn and Bacon.

Morgan, D. P., & Jenson, W. R. (1988). *Teaching behaviorally disordered students: Preferred practices.* Columbus, OH: Merrill.

Morgan, S. R., & Reinhart, J. A. (1991). *Interventions for students with emotional disorders.* Austin, TX: ProEd.

Northwest Regional Educational Laboratory. (1984). *Effective schooling practices: A research synthesis.* Portland, OR: Goal-Based Educational Program.

Sugai, G., & Colvin, G. (1989). *Environmental explanations of behavior: Conducting a functional analysis.* Eugene, OR: Behavior Associates.

Walker, H. M., McConnell, S., Holmes, D., Todis, B., Walker, J., & Golden, N. (1983). *The Walker social skills curriculum: The ACCEPTS program.* Austin, TX: Pro-Ed.

Walker, J. E., & Shea, T. M. (1980). *Behavior modification: A practical approach for educators* (2nd ed.). St. Louis: Mosby.

Wolery, M., Bailey, D. B., Jr., & Sugai, G. M. (1988). *Effective teaching: Principles and procedures of applied behavior analysis with exceptional students.* Boston: Allyn and Bacon.

Zionts, P. (1985). *Teaching disturbed and disturbing students.* Austin, TX: Pro-Ed.

3. Collaboration for Success

Cooperative arrangements are essential in educational endeavors in which the human service system has outgrown its direct service capabilities (Friend, 1988). For professional survival, as well as for maximum student benefit, the teacher of students with behavioral disorders must initiate cooperative working arrangements with other special education teachers, regular education teachers, administrators, support personnel, and parents. Successful collaboration is the sum of two crucial components: communication and resources. This section highlights strategies for enhancing and optimizing both by addressing questions related to professional collaboration and parent involvement.

Collaborating with Other Teachers and Paraprofessionals

What are some effective strategies for developing good working relationships?

Teachers of students with behavioral disorders must master the art of public relations. It is not uncommon for special education teachers who work with students with BD to be viewed with the same suspicion and distrust as their students. Teachers need to become skilled at presenting themselves as nonthreatening individuals and communicate a willingness to collaborate with others. Teachers of students with BD will find themselves initiating contact with other teachers the majority of the time. Most interactions with other personnel will be brief, but the power of a quick, positive comment should not be underestimated. Following is a list of strategies teachers of students with BD can use to develop effective working relationships with regular education staff:

- Make positive comments on activities and products that are observed in regular education classrooms. Request copies of materials currently used in the regular education classroom for use in the special education classroom.

- Notice themes and topics of study in regular education classrooms; suggest materials or ideas that have been successful in the special education classroom and might complement the regular education curriculum.

- Be a ready listener for colleagues. Avoid becoming the "campus therapist," but listening and suggesting strategies can promote camaraderie.

How can teachers of students with behavioral disorders increase regular staff understanding?

Do not expect regular education staff to request information about these students. If there is a need to increase the regular school staff's understanding of the characteristics and needs of students with behavioral disorders, responsibility often falls to the special education teacher. Some effective ways of disseminating information about students with BD include the following:

- Make copies of fact sheets and media items concerning the education of students with behavioral problems for distribution among the staff. Provide a name and room number contact for further discussion. If copying capacity is limited, post the information in a high-visibility spot (e.g., entrance to lounge, next to soda machine) and update the information frequently.

- Display willingness to discuss the characteristics of students with behavioral disorders for regular class teachers who have such students in their classes. Keep the presentation short, and be conscious of the rights and feelings of students with behavioral disorders. It is better to describe fictitious scenarios to promote understanding and tolerance rather than cite students by name. A series of individual discussions is often more effective than an assembly-type presentation.

- Look for opportunities to take *a few minutes* of time at faculty meetings to highlight effective management tips or current research in the field.

- Solicit input. Identify a few skills that have been targeted for certain students and ask for reports of positive "sightings." Focus on the importance of having the entire staff catch the students being successful.

How can mainstreaming be achieved?

In most settings, it will be a long time before regular education is in favor of integration for children with behavioral problems. Special education teachers may meet opposition more often than they find support. With this in mind, set out to change a few attitudes at a time. Select two to four teachers who can best facilitate the mainstreaming needs of students with behavioral disorders and work to develop their cooperation. Ways to promote positive attitudes toward mainstreaming should include the following:

- Model effective interaction behaviors that should be displayed when interacting with students with behavioral disorders.

- Ascertain that the mainstream is ready for students with behavioral disorders before integration. Work with the regular education teacher to establish specific behavioral contingencies (try to focus on positives) and determine that the mainstream class is ready to tolerate potential differences.

- Equip students with "teacher-pleasing" behaviors. Conduct environmental analyses to pinpoint which behaviors different teachers deem essential for success. Teach these skills to the student with BD.

- Maintain contact with the teacher and class after mainstreaming has occurred. If support is withdrawn once the integration goal has been accomplished, and problems arise, future mainstreaming efforts may be met with resistance.

- Be willing to engage in team teaching. Offer to teach the entire mainsteam class to demonstrate effective and desirable teaching practices.

How can the teacher of students with behavioral disorders effectively assist the regular education teacher?

Effective educational interventions for students with behavioral disorders require teamwork that is based on open communication and a pooling of resources. Not only will teamwork maximize student outcomes, but job satisfaction and teacher health will be enhanced. Collaboration demands a shift from the idea of periodic consultation to the concept of ongoing shared responsibility and shared accountability. Underscoring successful collaboration is a mutual sense of respect and a willingness to share negative experiences as well as positive ones. Sometimes the most valuable information that can be shared with other staff is a description of interventions that have failed. Making use of the suggestions, strategies, and techniques provided here will enable the teacher of students with behavioral disorders to competently assist other staff. Other mechanisms to ensure effective assistance include

- Setting up formal teacher assistance teams.

- Providing a time when teachers can meet regularly to discuss concerns.

- Providing to the regular education staff, on a regular basis, information and options concerning possible effective instructional strategies.

Collaborating with Administrators

What can be done to increase the awareness of administrators, legislators, and the community?

Communication and identification of mutually beneficial activities will promote awareness of and support for the needs of students with behavioral disorders. Although the methods of communication may differ somewhat, all three of the intended audiences should be made aware of the strengths and potential of students with BD. Have a clear goal and specific suggestions ready for those times when information is requested. Opportunities to interact with administrators typically are encountered daily. After each interaction, be sure to reinforce any positive effort made by the administrator. Mentioning students' accomplishments and how increased support would further benefit students—and in turn the school—may promote future efforts by administrators for the benefit of students with BD. Remember, the major motivation for support lies in mutual benefit. If all else fails, the prospect of improved school functioning may capture administrators' attention. To promote awareness on the part of the administrators, legislators, and the community,

- Extend invitations to administrators, government officials, and community resource persons to visit BD classes. Make it a positive experience for the students so that they will anticipate visits eagerly.

- Generate correspondence from the students to officials. Writing to civic leaders can be accomplished under the auspices of units on democracy, civil rights, making requests, civic responsibility, and so forth. Leaders will be unable to ignore contacts from potential future constituents and the accompanying public relations opportunities.

What skills do teachers need to deal effectively with administrative requests?

Employment brings with it a certain amount of conformity. However, by developing the ability to be effective communicators, teachers can avoid petty misunderstandings and be assertive in defining developmental needs. Teachers should be confident about their abilities and realize that administrative decisions are often influenced by financial constraints and not by the teachers' qualities or abilities. In dealing with administrative requests, teachers should

- Identify the important element on which to focus energy. Not all requests will be met, so it is better to concentrate on the essential needs.
- Be proactive by keeping administrators posted of new developments in the field of behavioral disorders.
- Send administrators written correspondence related to outcomes with certain class sizes or documentation of what can be accomplished with the support of full-time assistants.
- Make a deliberate effort to compliment administrators' contributions as they relate to exemplary practice.

What can be done when the budget falls short?

There will probably never be enough money to provide ideal programming. Budget constraints force teacher creativity. Teachers should collaborate with other professionals, community groups, advocates, and parents to piece together a desired program. Often programs that must be developed with little or no financial support are more time consuming, but are of higher quality because they reflect joint efforts.

Collaborating with the Community

How can a support network be established?

Teachers who present themselves as advocates for students with behavioral disorders will discover that community leaders may seek them for information. Teachers can magnify efforts by identifying team members who will take responsibility for getting in touch with representatives of various agencies. A little time spent at the beginning of the year to identify contacts will facilitate networking later. To facilitate the establishment of a support network, the teacher can

- Consider networks that are already established, checking with social workers and home-school coordinators to determine their resources.
- Identify agencies at the local, state, and national levels. Most will have directories of services that they will mail to teachers.
- Compile a list of names and phone numbers of community social service resources for students and families. These will vary depending on the student's age and need. It is important to remember that the teacher is not making a referral, but simply providing options for resources.

What happens when a student is arrested and incarcerated?

During incarceration, the student is the responsibility of the juvenile justice system. Teachers are limited in their responsibility and ability to provide educational interventions. Proactive planning documented in the educational program and a clear delineation of behaviors that are related to a disabling condition will enable the teacher to determine when the student's behaviors have become a clear and present danger. Even though incarcerated, the student is entitled to continue receiving special education services. The agencies responsible for ensuring that services are provided may vary. For example, in Texas, the Texas Youth Commission must continue to provide educational services to identified special education youth.

Collaborating with Parents

Where can teachers refer parents who seek help in working with their children?

In most districts, teachers may not refer parents to nonschool entities, such as counseling, because of the financial obligation implied. However, teachers can provide a list of resource options. Teachers should

- Compile a resource list including services such as parent support groups, social service agencies, hotline numbers, federally funded projects, and health and human services systems.

- Encourage parents to identify their needs and match them to the appropriate agency.

What communication techniques facilitate good parent/teacher relationships?

Parent communication can be enhanced with the same techniques found to be successful with other colleagues. Parents will tend to be more willing to communicate with teachers who present themselves as active, empathetic, and *nonjudgmental* listeners. To facilitate the process, the teacher should

- Establish a forum for *frequent* communication with the parent. Emphasize positives in a brief fashion. One method is to use notebooks that are sent home to be returned the next day. It will take time and patience to establish such a routine; the students themselves may present initial resistance. The teacher might also try making a telephone call once a week to each family to relate positive information as well as areas of concern.

- Communicate using the same vocabulary and level of understanding as the parents. Clearly lay out class expectations and school rules (dress, language, etc.), but be aware of and sensitive to differing parental expectations or cultural norms.

- Acknowledge parents' other commitments and suggest ideas for involvement that are easy and convenient for them.

- Spend time outside of the IEP meeting on common goal setting. Everyone will be concerned with the student's postschool transitions, so make goals relevant to that end. Parents will be more cooperative if they are motivated by more than just the student's school functioning.

How can teachers promote the generalization of positive change into the home environment?

The key to promoting generalization is effective communication. To enhance the effort the teacher can

- Define and describe techniques used in school. Facilitate the parents' abilities to use the same methods by presenting them in detail with examples relevant for home use.

- Follow up on the parents' actions during the school day.

- Encourage the development of parent education programs to provide the parents with a full range of strategies for managing behavior and motivating their children.

- Ensure that the behavioral expectations can be transferred to the home environment feasibly.

How can the educational system meet the needs of students given the restraints of a difficult home life?

Although most parents care deeply about their children, there are some who have neither the capacity nor the ability to raise their children effectively. Teachers have control over only the student's school behaviors. Realizing this, the teacher can focus school activities to encourage and promote adaptive behavioral changes outside of school. If it is suspected that the student comes from a dysfunctional family, the teacher can talk with the school social worker or home-school coordinator to suggest family support services. Whenever possible, the teacher should avoid being put in an adversarial role against the parents. The teacher should be aware of and reinforce the family's efforts in working with their child.

Related Reading

Berger, E. H. (1987). *Parents as partners in education: The school and home working together* (2nd ed.). Columbus, OH: Merrill.

Conoley, J. C. (1986). Serving special children through teacher consultation. In C. L. Warger & L. E. Addinger (Eds.), *Preparing special educators for teacher consultation* (pp. 1–17). Toledo, OH: University of Toledo.

Friend, M. (1988). Putting consultation into context: Historical and contemporary perspectives. *Remedial and Special Education, 9*(6), 7–13.

Idol, L., Paolucci-Whitcomb, P., & Nevin, A. (1986). *Collaborative consultation*. Rockville, MD: Aspen.

Johnson, L. J., Pugach, M. C., & Devlin, S. (1990). Professional collaboration. *TEACHING Exceptional Children, 22*(2), 9–11.

Phillips, V., & McCullough, L. (1990). Consultation-based programming: Instituting the collaborative ethic in schools. *Exceptional Children, 56*, 291–304.

Polsgrove, L., & McNeil, M. (1989). The consultative process: Research and practice. *Remedial and Special Education, 10*(1), 6–13.

CEC Mini-Library
Working with Behavioral Disorders

Edited by Lyndal M. Bullock and Robert B. Rutherford, Jr.

A set of nine books developed with the practitioner in mind.

Use this Mini-Library as a reference to help staff understand the problems of specific groups of youngsters with behavioral problems.

- *Teaching Students with Behavioral Disorders: Basic Questions and Answers.* Timothy J. Lewis, Juane Heflin, & Samuel A. DiGangi. No. P337. 1991. 37 pages.

- *Conduct Disorders and Social Maladjustments: Policies, Politics, and Programming.* Frank H. Wood, Christine O. Cheney, Daniel H. Cline, Kristina Sampson, Carl R. Smith, & Eleanor C. Guetzloe. No. P338. 1991. 27 pages.

- *Behaviorally Disordered? Assessment for Identification and Instruction.* Bob Algozzine, Kathy Ruhl, & Roberta Ramsey, No. P339. 1991. 37 pages.

- *Preparing to Integrate Students with Behavioral Disorders.* Robert A. Gable, Virginia K. Laycock, Sharon A. Maroney, & Carl R. Smith. No. P340. 1991. 35 pages

- *Teaching Young Children with Behavioral Disorders.* Mary Kay Zabel. No. P341. 1991. 25 pages.

- *Reducing Undesirable Behaviors.* Edited by Lewis Polsgrove. No. P342. 1991. 33 pages.

- *Social Skills for Students with Autism.* Richard L. Simpson, Brenda Smith Myles, Gary M. Sasso, & Debra M. Kamps. No. P343. 1991. 23 pages.

- *Special Education in Juvenile Corrections.* Peter E. Leone, Robert B. Rutherford, Jr., & C. Michael Nelson. No. P344. 1991. 26 pages.

- *Moving On: Transitions for Youth with Behavioral Disorders.* Michael Bullis & Robert Gaylord-Ross. No. P345. 1991. 52 pages.

Save 10% by ordering the entire library, No. P346, 1991. Call for the most current price information, 703/264-9467.

Send orders to:
The Council for Exceptional Children, Dept. K10350
1920 Association Drive, Reston VA 22091-1589